To

From

Date

GLORIA COPELAND

THE
SECRET PLACE
GOD'S
PROTECTION

KENNETH
COPELAND
PUBLICATIONS

The Secret Place of God's Protection

ISBN-10 1-57562-672-1   30-0601
ISBN-13 978-1-57562-672-7

12 11 10 09 08 07   8 7 6 5 4 3

© 2002 Eagle Mountain International Church Inc. aka Kenneth Copeland Publications

Kenneth Copeland Publications
Fort Worth, TX 76192-0001

For more information about Kenneth Copeland Ministries, call 800-600-7395 or visit www.kcm.org.

KCP Records
The Music of Ministry

Produced, Engineered and Mixed by: Win Kutz
Assisted by: Leland Bennett and Michael Howell
Edited by: Michael Howell
Arranged by: Jerry Cleveland
Keyboards: Jerry Cleveland
Percussion: Jim DeLong
Lead Vocals: Len Mink
Background Vocalists: Paul Smith, Don Wallace, Karen Cruise Adams, Michael Howell

Special Thanks To: Kenneth and Gloria Copeland

One OF THE MOST IMPORTANT THINGS I EVER LEARNED  was to stand on Psalm 91 for protection. I put it in my heart from *The Amplified Bible,* and that is the version I use for my own protection. So I am going to quote extensively from that, as well as from other scriptures on protection.

Here is what the Lord told me when I first began to teach on this many years ago:

There is a place in Christ Jesus where we abide in the secret place of God's protection. The world knows nothing about this secret place, nor can they live there. It is a place revealed by the Holy Spirit through the Word of God. It is for the obedient. Our life is hid with Christ in God.

You too can learn how to abide in that secret place. It's available to every believer. You don't have to be afraid or worried about tomorrow. Security, protection and peace of mind belong to you. They are your covenant rights in Christ Jesus.

Gloria Copeland

HE WHO DWELLS

IN THE SECRET PLACE OF THE MOST HIGH

shall remain stable and fixed under the shadow of the Almighty [Whose power no foe can withstand].

I will say of the Lord, He is my Refuge and my Fortress, my God; on Him I lean and rely, and in Him I [confidently] trust!

For [then] He will deliver you from the snare of the fowler and from the deadly pestilence.

[Then] He will cover you with His pinions, and under His wings shall you trust and find refuge; His truth and His faithfulness are a shield and a buckler.

You shall not be afraid of the terror of the night, nor of the arrow (the evil plots and slanders of the wicked) that flies by day, nor of the pestilence that stalks in darkness, nor of the destruction and sudden death that surprise and lay waste at noonday.

A thousand may fall at your side, and ten thousand at your right hand, but it shall not come near you.

Only a spectator shall you be [yourself inaccessible in the secret place of the Most High] as you witness the reward of the wicked.

Because you have made the Lord your refuge, and the Most High your dwelling place, there shall no evil befall you, nor any plague or calamity come near your tent.

For He will give His angels [especial] charge over you to accompany and defend and preserve you in all your ways [of obedience and service]. They shall bear you up on their hands, lest you dash your foot against a stone.

You shall tread upon the lion and adder; the young lion and the serpent shall you trample underfoot.

Because he has set his love upon Me, therefore will I deliver him; I will set him on high, because he knows and understands My name [has a personal knowledge of My mercy, love, and kindness—trusts and relies on Me, knowing I will never forsake him, no, never].

He shall call upon Me, and I will answer him; I will be with him in trouble, I will deliver him and honor him.

With long life will I satisfy him and show him My salvation.

Psalm 91 | *THE AMPLIFIED BIBLE*

Believing God's Word opens the door for His supernatural help and for the angels of God to minister on your behalf.

Unbelief opens the door to the devil and evil spirits that cause bad things to come to pass in your life. You're either giving the devil something to work with or you're giving God something to work with.

GOD
WATCHES

In Deuteronomy 30:19, God said, *"I have set before you life and death, blessing and cursing, therefore choose life...."* Choose the Word of God.

Keep the Word about your protection going in your eyes and in your ears until you get it down into your heart, until it overtakes your natural thoughts or maybe the way you've been raised all your life. Take the Word of God and break the habit of saying words that rob you of your angelic protection. Your life depends on it, and it is certainly well worth any effort to do it.

Go over Psalm 91 every day. It wouldn't hurt you to go over it and deliverance scriptures every day the rest of your life. Do it until His care for you gets so big in you that unbelief and fear have absolutely no place in your life.

GLORIA COPELAND

OVER YOU

God said to Moses when He was showing him His glory, *"There is a place by me"* (Exodus 33:21). We have a secret place. It is a place where Satan has no access. Terror has no access. Glory to God! There is a place for us by God, in God, that is fully protected.

It thrills me that I don't have to be afraid of death! I don't have to be afraid of anything in this life. Scripture asks if God is for me, who can be against me? (Romans 8:31).

In this secret place, you know that you are not in any trouble because there is nothing higher than the Most High! He can't be outdone, overcome, run over or put down.

There is no higher place to dwell than in the Most High.

GLORIA
COPELAND

THE
SECRET

He who dwells in the secret place of the Most High shall remain stable and fixed under the shadow of the Almighty [Whose power no foe can withstand].

PSALM 91:1
THE AMPLIFIED BIBLE

PLACE

He that dwelleth in the secret place of the most High

shall abide under the shadow of the Almighty.

PSALM 91:1

Lord, You have been our

dwelling place & our refuge

in all generations....

PSALM 90:1, *THE AMPLIFIED BIBLE*

STAY

J esus said in John 15:7, *"If ye abide in me, and my words abide in you, ye shall ask what ye will, and it shall be done unto you."* That word *abide* means "to dwell, to stay, to remain."

You abide in the secret place not by continually coming and going in and out, but by staying *"fixed under the shadow of the Almighty,"* as *The Amplified Bible* says. You stay in contact with God—you stay close—so you hear and obey God when He talks to you.

The word *dwell* says to us, "This man or woman is devoted to God." This person doesn't live for God one day, then go out in the world the next doing things they shouldn't. They're not in the group of people who go to church every once in a while, who honor God when they think about it, and who give on occasion. They obey God and spend enough time with Him to know what

it takes to obey Him and to walk in His ways. They honor His Word.

If you want to be guaranteed a safe life, stay in that place of refuge. Abide in that place of refuge. Make that your dwelling place.

Don't be coming in and going out. Don't be on fire for a little while, then cool off, go do other things, and forget about Him. No! Stay attached to God, and remain stable and fixed under the shadow of the Almighty.

G LORIA COPELAND

IN TOUCH

Teach me thy way, O Lord, and lead me in a plain path, because of mine enemies. 〰 PSALM 27:11

Trust in the Lord with all thine heart; and lean not unto thine own understanding. In all thy ways acknowledge him, and he shall direct thy paths. 〰 PROVERBS 3:5-6

my

fortress

IN YOU, O LORD, I PUT MY

TRUST...DELIVER ME SPEEDILY;

BE MY ROCK OF REFUGE, A FORTRESS

OF DEFENSE TO SAVE ME. FOR YOU

ARE MY ROCK AND MY FORTRESS;

THEREFORE, FOR YOUR NAME'S SAKE,

LEAD ME AND GUIDE ME.

PSALM 31:1–3
NEW KING JAMES VERSION

thine heart

If we want to be protected and enjoy all the *protection* that belongs to us, we have to live our lives *listening—as a habit.*

FOLLOW THE

Don't wait and think, *Well if I get in trouble God will tell me, and I'll just ignore Him all the rest of the time.* No, to stay in that secret place of protection, listen to correction. Maintain a lifestyle of having an ear to God, listening down in your heart to direction and leading.

Be *pliable.*

A dear friend said it this way: We have to be like a log going through the water. A log will go down the river, and it will follow the current. Wherever the current goes, that's where that log is willing to go.

If you will listen and act when God speaks, you will be easy to move. God will put you in the right place at the right time, doing the right thing, if you'll just be pliable. Be quick to hear and obey. Don't be set in your ways. Be willing to be moved and changed.

GLORIA COPELAND

THE STEPS OF A GOOD MAN
ARE ORDERED BY THE LORD....
PSALM 37:23

A COUPLE OF YEARS AGO AFTER SOME CRISES HAD HIT THE COUNTRY, I WAS THINKING ABOUT THE TERRIBLE THINGS THAT GO ON IN THE WORLD. THE LORD SAID TO ME ONE DAY,

Set

Separate yourself and you will be separated.

What did He mean by that? He meant we are to separate ourselves from the darkness, the evil, the sin and negative ways. Separate ourselves from unbelieving ways, from the darkness of this world unto Him.

In fact, that's what the word *holy* means—separate. If we are a holy people, we are a people who have been taken out of the world and separated unto God by the new birth.

So we let God separate us from the old way of life by renewing our minds. Romans 12 says that the renewing of our minds is what transforms us and places us in the good and the perfect will of God. In the perfect will of God, there is nothing missing, nothing broken.

> *Wherefore come out from among them, and be ye separate, saith the Lord, and touch not the unclean thing; and I will receive you, and will be a Father unto you...*
>
> 2 CORINTHIANS 6:17-18

In other words, He is saying, "Give Me an opportunity and I will show you what a father is really like. Give me an opportunity by hearing Me and doing what I say, and I will manifest Myself to you, and I will be a father to you."

GLORIA COPELAND

apart *to be loved*

Nothing
NOTHING

You will guard him and keep him

in perfect and constant peace whose

mind [both its inclination and its

character] is stayed on You....

ISAIAH 26:3
THE AMPLIFIED BIBLE

And the very God of peace sanctify you wholly; and I pray God your whole spirit and

Missing
BROKEN

The word in the Hebrew for peace, *shalom,* means "nothing missing, nothing broken." (It is also translated *prosperity.)* It means the same as the word "salvation" in the New Testament.

Salvation is more than just being born again. It is deliverance from every kind of evil, and from fear. It means wholeness or soundness and includes prosperity.

The word *wholly* in 1 Thessalonians 5:23 in the *King James Version* means "whole, complete, undamaged and intact." In fact, I make that a part of my prayer. I just say, "Lord, I thank You for keeping me whole and complete, undamaged and intact all the days of my life." *Preserved* in that same verse means "to watch over or keep." It has a sense of protection or watching over.

Peace and wholeness are what God wants in your life—spirit and soul and body. We have a covenant which includes all these things.

We have a covenant of peace—nothing missing, nothing broken.

GLORIA COPELAND

For though the mountains should depart and the hills be shaken or removed,

yet My love and kindness shall not depart from you, nor shall My covenant of

peace and completeness be removed, says the Lord....

ISAIAH 54:10, *THE AMPLIFIED BIBLE*

...oul and body be preserved blameless unto the coming of our Lord Jesus Christ.
1 THESSALONIANS 5:23

> *Where is the man who fears the Lord? God will teach him how to choose the best. He shall live within God's circle of blessing…*
>
> PSALM 25:12-13
> *THE LIVING BIBLE*

LIFE IS GOOD IN GOD'S CIRCLE OF BLESSING.

When we put our relationship with God first place, we will live in a circle of blessing that no devil can penetrate, no worldly situation or circumstance can overcome, and no enemy can break down.

The blessing in Deuteronomy 28 is that our enemies will flee before us. No enemy can stand before us. Every sickness and disease is under the curse.

In God's circle of blessing, we live well. Our bodies are blessed. Our children are blessed. Our relationships are blessed. Even our property and possessions are blessed. Life is good in God's circle of blessing.

GLORIA COPELAND

THE *Circle* OF

Say this: *I'm living in God's circle of blessing. Whichever way I turn, there is blessing. I have a circle of blessing around me. Everywhere I go, that circle goes with me. It's not in circumstances. It's around me. Where I go the blessing goes. It's in my heart, in my relationship with the Lord.*

I'm believing God. I'm walking with God. I'm expecting God to do great and mighty things. I'm obeying God. He is number one. I seek Him first. I listen to Him first.

BLESSING

For verily I say unto you, That whosoever

shall...not doubt in his heart, but shall believe

that those things which he saith shall come

to pass; he shall have whatsoever he saith.

MARK 11:23

I will say of th

I will say of the Lord, He is my Refuge
and my Fortress, my God; on Him I lean
and rely, and in Him I [confidently] trust!

PSALM 91:2, *THE AMPLIFIED BIBLE*

According to Romans 10, faith has to be in two places—in your heart and in your mouth. Your protection is the same. You have to say of the Lord He is your refuge. You have to take refuge in Him. You have to exercise your faith for these things based on what you see in the Word of God.

Those who would stay and abide in the shadow of the Almighty are the ones who will *say,* "The Lord is my refuge!" They make the Lord their refuge, and they won't be talked out of it.

You see, our part is staying under His shadow, trusting Him and *saying.* Saying words of deliverance. Saying words of freedom—not of fear or of trouble.

You've made Jesus your Savior. You've made Jesus your Healer. Now make Him your refuge and keep Him in that place in your thoughts and in your words.

Say, "God is my refuge. Jesus has redeemed me from the curse" (Deuteronomy 28). The curse would be anything bad. Jesus has redeemed you from it.

Stay attached to God, in that place of the Most High where your security, your deliverance and your salvation are. Stay there with your words and with your actions.

Lord

GLORIA COPELAND

faith
IS NOT
SILENT

We having the same spirit of faith, according as it is written, I believed, and therefore have I spoken; we also believe, and therefore speak.
2 CORINTHIANS 4:13

I believed, therefore have I spoken...
PSALM 116:1

I believe

The spirit of faith is not silent. It doesn't go in for silent prayer or silent confession. The spirit of faith believes and it speaks. We have to take God as our refuge, our fortress and our protector the same way we took Him as our Savior.

Abide under the shadow of the Almighty and *say* "The Lord is my refuge" like you *said* "He's my Savior and my healer." Then you will be in position to be protected.

What are you doing? You're releasing your faith for that. You're saying words of faith to give Him place in your life.

You are taking your place in that covenant protection.

We have to take God as our refuge, our fortress and our protector the same way we took Him as our Savior.

SAY THIS: "He is my God. He is my refuge. I trust Him, I lean upon Him, I believe in Him."

GLORIA COPELAND

The fear of man bringeth a snare: but whoso putteth his trust in the Lord shall be safe. PROVERBS 29:25

*T*RUST *in the*

...My God; on Him I lean and rely, and in Him I [confidently] trust!

PSALM 91:2
THE AMPLIFIED BIBLE

But the salvation of the righteous is of

the Lord: he is their strength in the time

of trouble. And the Lord shall help them,

and deliver them: he shall deliver them

from the wicked, and save them, because

they trust in him. PSALM 37:39-40

What gets you delivered is not talking fear and letting fear come in to rule you and dominate you. It is having the Word of God in your heart and saying it. It is trusting Him with your life.

GLORIA COPELAND

Thank You,

THANK YOU FOR EVERY TIME *You delivered us* WHEN WE DIDN'T EVEN KNOW WE WERE IN DANGER.

for delivering the people of God. Thank You that no harm shall come to us. I plead the blood of Jesus over me and over my loved ones. I thank You for protecting our homes and our families.

Thank You for every time You delivered us when we didn't even know we were in danger. Thank You for those times that we knew we were in trouble and You brought us out.

We abide under the shadow of Your wings, Lord, under the shadow of the Almighty. We trust in You. We say, "You are our refuge and our fortress, our God, and in You do we confidently trust."

To You be all the glory, Lord. *Amen.*

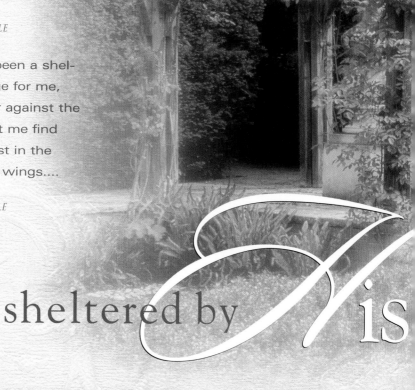

[Then] He will cover you
with His pinions, and
under His wings shall you
trust and find refuge....

PSALM 91:4
THE AMPLIFIED BIBLE

For You have been a shel-
ter and a refuge for me,
a strong tower against the
adversary....Let me find
refuge and trust in the
shelter of Your wings....

PSALM 61:3-4
THE AMPLIFIED BIBLE

sheltered by *His*

When Jesus looked out at Jerusalem, He said, *"How often I wanted to gather your children together, as a hen gathers her chicks under her wings, but you were not willing!"* (Matthew 23:37, *New King James Version*).

Have you ever seen a mother hen gather her chicks? She will spread out her wings and pull her little chicks in underneath, and she'll totally cover them with her wings.

That is what God does for us—He covers us. I'm talking about being covered with the power of God. It's not just a shadow or cloud *above* you, but it's a cloud *around* you. It's the presence of God *around* you.

I've thought about the shelter. I've thought about the refuge. I've thought about the feathers covering us. And until recently, I saw them mostly like the shelter of a roof. But I am seeing more clearly than ever that when He says He covers you, it is more like the way a mother hen takes care of her chicks.

He covers you from the top of your head to the soles of your feet.

GLORIA COPELAND

Be merciful unto me, O God, be merciful unto me: for my soul trusteth in thee: yea, in the shadow of thy wings will I make my refuge.... PSALM 57:1

wings

inoculate
yourself

He will deliver you from the snare of the fowler and from the deadly pestilence. ❧ PSALM 91:3, *THE AMPLIFIED BIBLE*

You shall not be afraid of...the pestilence that stalks in darkness.... ❧ PSALM 91:5-6, *THE AMPLIFIED BIBLE*

I n Luke 21:11, *The Amplified Bible* says the word *pestilence* means, "plagues: malignant and contagious or infectious epidemic diseases which are deadly and devastating."

Pestilence is not for you. You can inocu-late your family with Psalm 91.

Soon after the New York City terrorist attack September 11, 2001, Ken said, "I want all the kids to come over to the house tonight." So we called all of our children and grandchildren for a family meeting. We took our inoculation with God's Word for any kind of plague or anything that would try to come in our water, in our air, on our bodies—however it would come. Everything that anybody could dream up, anything any terrorist could do, was covered with the blood. We took Communion that night and covered it with the blood.

> *Pestilence is not for you. You can inoculate your family with Psalm 91.*

Now, we had done the same thing once during the flu epidemic when the children were small. We gathered the family together and said, "We are going to have a flu shot." John's eyes opened wide as saucers. He wasn't sure he wanted a flu shot. But we took it with the Word of God. We took it with Psalm 91. By the way, we've never had the flu!

Psalm 91 is always up-to-date. You can't come up with anything that is not covered by it.

*G*LORIA COPELAND

THE *Glory*

But let all those who take refuge and put their trust in You rejoice; let them ever sing and shout for joy, because You make a covering over them and defend them…. You, Lord, will bless the [uncompromisingly] righteous [him who is upright and in right standing with You]; as with a shield You will surround him….

PSALM 5:11-12, *THE AMPLIFIED BIBLE*

of the Lord

will be your rear guard.

ISAIAH 58:8

...He is a shield to those who trust and take refuge in Him. ❧ PROVERBS 30:5, *THE AMPLIFIED BIBLE*

For in the day of trouble He will hide me in His shelter; in the secret place of His tent will He hide me; He will set me high upon a rock. ❧ PSALM 27:5, *THE AMPLIFIED BIBLE*

See yourself encircled with the power of God, the protection of God, the presence of God, the glory of God. Being separated unto the Lord, fully living for Him, puts you in a place of protection where the anointing of God and the power of God is your rear guard.

Guarded

Scripture records that the pillar of cloud leading the children of Israel in their exodus moved from the front of the group to the back of the group and was Israel's rear guard (see Exodus 14:19).

Glory to God. We're guarded from the front. We're guarded from the back. We're guarded on every side.

GLORIA COPELAND

Lord, I thank You that I am surrounded

by Your favor. You totally cover me

on every side

about, encompassing me with favor as

with a shield. Thank You that I am

shielded. I am protected. *Amen.*

Surely OR ONLY *goodness,*

And I have put My words in your mouth and have covered you

with the shadow of My hand.... ISAIAH 51:16, *THE AMPLIFIED BIBLE*

mercy,
&unfailing love

The Lord
is good to all:
and his tender
mercies are
over all
his works.

PSALM 145:9

shall follow me all the days of my life,

and through the length of my days the

house of the Lord [and His presence]

shall be my dwelling place.

PSALM 23:6, *THE AMPLIFIED BIBLE*

Many years ago when John was a teenager in high school, I was concerned about him. All boy, he just did what the other boys did. He turned things over. He wrecked his truck. He wrecked motorcycles. He wrecked the Jeep. He wrecked go-carts. And walked away from every one. I was concerned he wouldn't live long enough to grow up and mature.

I had him on my heart one day 10,000 miles away in Australia, and God spoke to Ken in the airplane. Ken turned to me and said, "I got a word from the Lord. He said, *My mercy hovers over John.*"

That set me free. Five words the Lord gave us that day set me free forever concerning John and his outcome.

God was saying to me, "Don't worry about John. I am hovering over him. My mercy hovers over your boy. I'm going to stay right with him until things are just right in his life. I'm going to stay right with him until he grows up and matures. I'm going to keep his life."

I appreciated that so much. The truth is that God's mercy hovers over all of us like that if we make Him our refuge with faith that speaks our salvation.

God's mercy, His shadow, His hand is hovering over you and your children all the time ready to be received. We have His Word!

GLORIA COPELAND

mercy HOVERS

HID WITH CHRIST IN GOD

...Your life is hid

We have a place to live that is protected and sure. We have a secret place to live in Christ Jesus. It's a place not available outside of faith in Him—a place that is offered to everyone who will trust in Him.

Our life is hid with Christ in God.

*GLORIA
COPELAND*

You are a hiding place for me; You, Lord, preserve me from trouble, You surround me with songs and shouts of deliverance....

PSALM 32:7, *THE AMPLIFIED BIBLE*

You are my hiding place and my shield; I hope in Your word.

PSALM 119:114, *THE AMPLIFIED BIBLE*

Keep and guard me as the pupil of Your eye; hide me in the shadow of Your wings.

PSALM 17:8, *THE AMPLIFIED BIBLE*

Oh, how great is Your goodness, which You have laid up for those who fear, revere, and worship You, goodness which You have wrought for those who trust and take refuge in You before the sons of men! In the secret place of Your presence You hide them from the plots of men; You keep them secretly in Your pavilion....

PSALM 31:19–20, *THE AMPLIFIED BIBLE*

with Christ in God. ❧ COLOSSIANS 3:3

But the Lord is faithful; he will make you strong
and guard you from satanic attacks of every kind.

2 THESSALONIANS 3:3, *THE LIVING BIBLE*

NO GAPS IN

Think about what the shield and buckler are for.

Jesus said, *"The truth shall make you free"* (John 8:32). The Word of God is truth (John 17:17).

Scripture says, *"For the word of God is quick, and powerful, and sharper than any twoedged sword, piercing even to the dividing asunder of soul and spirit..."* (Hebrews 4:12). The Word of God in our mouths is our faith, and action comes because we speak the Word of God. It gives God place in our lives.

You have to know the truth before it can be your shield and buckler. You have to find out from the Word of God what God says about you. Then you can strap on that shield and strap on that buckler.

The Hebrew word for "buckler" is related to the Hebrew word that means "circle." It describes a piece of armor that totally surrounds its wearer. It makes a circle around him, enclosing him, covering him and leaving no gaps.

Keep your shield and armor in place by filling your heart and mouth with the promises of God's Word. The protection of God, your refuge, will cover you completely.

GLORIA COPELAND

...His truth and His faithfulness are a shield and a buckler.
PSALM 91:4, *THE AMPLIFIED BIBLE*

Sanctify them through thy truth: thy word is truth. ❧ JOHN 17:17

YOUR ARMOR

But the Lord is faithful, who shall stablish you, and keep you from evil.
2 THESSALONIANS 3:3

God is faithful (reliable,
trustworthy, and therefore
ever true to His promise, and
He can be depended on)....

1 CORINTHIANS 1:9
THE AMPLIFIED BIBLE

There is no fear in love; but perfect love casts out fear, because fear involves torment. But he who fears has not been made perfect in love.

1 JOHN 4:18
NEW KING JAMES VERSION

A MIND RULED BY

faith

For God has not given us a spirit of fear, but of

power and of love and of a sound mind.

2 TIMOTHY 1:7
NEW KING JAMES VERSION

Now you don't need to be afraid of the dark any

more, nor fear the dangers of the day;

nor dread the plagues of darkness,

nor disasters in the morning.

PSALM 91:5-6
THE LIVING BIBLE

It's not OK for you to live in fear. Fear is an evil spirit over which you have authority.

Rise up in that authority and tell fear, "No! I cast you out in Jesus' Name. You're not coming here! You're not living here in me! I will not have a spirit of fear. I have a spirit of power, of love and a sound mind. I refuse to fear!"

A fear-ruled mind is not a sound mind. A faith-ruled mind is a sound mind. It's a mind and a heart and a mouth that talks about God being our refuge.

Thank the Lord, you have protection! You can go through this life, even in this crazy world, and live without fear. Perfect love casts fear out.

GLORIA COPELAND

You shall not be afraid of the terror of the night, nor of the arrow
(the evil plots and slanders of the wicked) that flies by day, nor
of the pestilence that stalks in darkness, nor of the destruction and
sudden death that surprise and lay waste at noonday.

PSALM 91:5-6, *THE AMPLIFIED BIBLE*

Give fear no

The Bible tells us not to fear. It says not to be terrified when you hear these things.

A mind that is renewed by the Word of God—that God is our protection and our refuge—is a blessed mind. It is a peaceful mind. We are to let that mind be in us that was also in Christ Jesus.

If you can't watch the news without getting disturbed, don't watch it. Spend that time depositing words in your heart that will cause you to be one who sits in the shadow of the Most High.

There, sitting in the place of the Most High under His shadow, you won't be terrified by bad reports, because you won't let fear have a place to stay.

When terror, fear, a lie of the devil or bad news tries to come, speak to it.

Say, "No, I'm not having it that way! I'm not taking fear. I'm sitting in the secret place of the Most High. I'm protected. I'm watched over. The Lord is my Refuge!"

GLORIA COPELAND

Fear not [there is nothing to fear], for I am with you; do not look around you in terror and be dismayed, for I am your God. I will strengthen and harden you to difficulties, yes, I will help you; yes, I will hold you up and retain you with My [victorious] right hand of rightness and justice.... For I the Lord your God hold your right hand; I am the Lord, Who says to you, Fear not; I will help you!

ISAIAH 41:10, 13,
THE AMPLIFIED BIBLE

place to stay

And when you hear of wars and insurrections (disturbances, disorder, and confusion), do not become alarmed and panic-stricken and terrified....

—LUKE 21:9, *THE AMPLIFIED BIBLE*

A thousand may fall at your side,

and ten thousand at your right hand,

but it shall not come near you.

PSALM 91:7 ❧ *THE AMPLIFIED BIBLE*

Is any thing too hard for the Lord?

GENESIS 18:14

YOU WILL
REMAIN
Standing

God DOES MAKE A DIFFERENCE.

Whatever situation you may be in the middle of right now, God can deliver you out of it—one person out of a thousand, a family out of a city, a city out of a nation, a nation out of the world. When people believe Him, and look to Him, and let Him be their God, He can deliver.

If you are standing on the Word of God, and you are in the secret place of the Most High, you are going to be standing there when nobody else is left.

If eleven thousand and one people were standing together, and ten thousand were to fall on one side and one thousand fall on the other, God has the marvelous ability to assure that you remain standing. You are hidden in the secret place of the Most High and His protection is over you.

If it weren't written in the Bible, we might think it is just too good to be true. But is there anything too hard for God?

No. Regardless of what comes our way, we can dwell under the shadow of the Almighty and remain stable and fixed under that shadow.

No power, no foe can withstand the presence and the power of God.

Gloria COPELAND

Only a spectator shall you be

[yourself inaccessible in the secret place of the

Most High] as you witness the reward of the wicked.

PSALM 91:8 ❧ *THE AMPLIFIED BIBLE*

A refuge

...The strength and power of Christ (the Messiah) may rest (yes, may pitch a

The word *refuge* means "shelter or protection from danger or distress; that which shelters or protects from danger, distress or calamity; a stronghold which protects by its strength; or a sanctuary which secures safety by its sacredness; any place inaccessible to the enemy."

God puts a tent of Himself around us and makes us inaccessible to the enemy when we obey verse one and verse two of Psalm 91—when we *abide* and when we *say*.

GLORIA COPELAND

The Lord is my Light and my Salvation—whom shall I fear or dread? The Lord is the Refuge and Stronghold of my life—of whom shall I be afraid?...For in the day of trouble He will hide me in His shelter; in the secret place of His tent will He hide me.... ✥ PSALM 27:1, 5, *THE AMPLIFIED BIBLE*

# of protection

tent over and dwell) upon me! ✥ 2 CORINTHIANS 12:9, *THE AMPLIFIED BIBLE*

HIS *way,*

ONLY WITH YOUR EYES

SHALL YOU LOOK,

AND SEE THE REWARD

OF THE WICKED.

PSALM 91:8 ❧ *NEW KING JAMES VERSION*

THE BLESSED WAY

Many are the sorrows of the wicked, but he who trusts in, relies on, and confidently leans on the Lord shall be compassed about with mercy and with loving-kindness.

PSALM 32:10
THE AMPLIFIED BIBLE

The word *wicked* in the Hebrew is the word for "lawless." Those who act lawlessly, disobeying God and not walking in His ways, suffer with the lawless. But, those who go in His ways and walk in love, doing the things He says and shunning the actions that He says are sin, reap their deliverance.

So, when we study the Bible, let's not overlook the conditions. The "ifs" are there to link us to the blessings.

If you will diligently hearken unto the voice of the Lord, the Scripture says, then *"all these blessings shall come on thee."* If you don't hearken to the voice of the Lord, *"all these curses shall come upon thee"* (see Deuteronomy 28:2, 15). You can't make the blessing work if you're disobedient. "If" works for you or against you. It is your choice.

The truth is, God tells us in detail how to live. God's ways work blessing and He teaches us His ways. In Matthew 6, Jesus said, *"But seek ye first the kingdom of God, and his righteousness; and all these things shall be added unto you"* (Matthew 6:33).

We decide how much of God's goodness we get out of life. How? Simply by deciding how much we will do things His way.

GLORIA COPELAND

Because you have made the Lord your refuge, and the Most High your dwelling place,

But the Lord is my defense; and my God is the rock of my refuge. PSALM 94:22

In the fear of the Lord is strong confidence: and his children shall have a place of refuge. PROVERBS 14:26

The fear of the Lord leads to life, and he who has it will abide in satisfaction; he will not be visited with evil. PROVERBS 19:23 NEW KING JAMES VERSION

WALK SAFELY

there shall no evil befall you, nor any plague or calamity come near your tent.

PSALM 91:9–10 ❧ *THE AMPLIFIED BIBLE*

When can you stand and believe God for protection? When you make Him your refuge and when you obey Him.

To be under God's protection, simply let Him be God. Obey Him and walk in the light that you have, always seeking more light. Protection is for the obedient. It is for the man or woman of faith who believes God's Word and acts on it.

Those who fear God and reverence Him enjoy His marvelous protection. Honor Him enough to do what He says. Take refuge in Him.

GLORIA COPELAND

Say this: *"No evil shall befall me because I make the Lord God my Refuge, and I sit in the place of the Most High's dwelling! I take my place there! No evil shall befall me, nor any plague nor calamity come near my tent. My whole house is delivered!"*

IN THE LIGHT

Willing to be

I thank You, Lord, that You are my refuge and my dwelling place, and I stay in You. I stay in your dwelling place. Lord, I am not coming in and going out. I am going to stay right here. I am going to obey Your Word. I am going to look to You, and hear from You, and do the things You tell me to do.

I ask You, Lord, to show me how to attach myself to You in ways even greater than I ever have before. Show me things that I need to do in my life to shore myself up, to make my life more secure in You, to change things, to correct.

Lord, I am standing on Titus 2 that says it is the grace of God that teaches me to live godly in this present world. I am believing right now for the grace, for the favor of God to teach me to live godly.

I receive it as a privilege, Lord, that You would correct me. When You do, I won't get upset about it, and I won't get my feelings hurt. I will be grateful for it, because it is an honor and a privilege to walk with You and to have You correct me when I need it. Just show me any place in my life that is an opening for evil. I don't want to give the devil any foothold.

Open your heart up

right now to the Lord and talk to Him. Let Him know that you are willing and ready to change anything you need to. Ask Him to show you.

Stay in that safe place where no evil can befall you nor any plague or calamity come near your tent.

GLORIA COPELAND

Changed

God is our refuge and strength, a very

present help in trouble. ❧ PSALM 46:1

The Lord of hosts is with us; the God of

Jacob is our refuge…. ❧ PSALM 46:7

IN *abiding*

Weymouth's translation of 1 John 2:24-25 says, *"For yourselves, let the teaching which you have heard from the beginning abide within you. If that teaching does abide within you, you also will abide in the Son and in the Father."*

Abiding is obeying. That's where our protection is.

It is doing the Word that makes us free. Jesus said when we know the truth, the truth will make us free. When we continue in His word, we will be His disciples indeed (see John 8:31-32). Joshua was told to meditate in the Word day and night and get it in his heart and in his mouth so that he would do it. Then he would deal wisely and have good success (Joshua 1:8).

That is the way we live, and that is why we can live without fear...*"Because you have made the Lord your refuge, and the Most High your dwelling place...."*

GLORIA COPELAND

IS PROTECTION

And take the helmet of salvation, and the sword of the Spirit, which is the word of God. ❧ EPHESIANS 6:17

For the word of God is quick, and powerful, and sharper than any twoedged sword.... ❧ HEBREWS 4:12

AN *angelic* SECURITY FORCE

For He will give His angels [especial] charge over you to

accompany and defend and preserve you in all your ways

[of obedience and service]. They shall bear you up

on their hands, lest you dash your foot against a stone.

PSALM 91:11-12 ❧ *THE AMPLIFIED BIBLE*

Thank God we've got angels. We have an angelic security force around us.

I don't go anywhere without security. Every time I go to the grocery store, I have my A-Team with me. My Angel Team goes with me everywhere I go.

You have angels assigned to you. The angels are there to administrate for you, to be God's agents in protecting you and keeping you.

Be aware of your angels and do not bind them up with words contrary to your deliverance.

They can't act on words of fear and failure. If you say something that is counter to your deliverance and God providing for you, they just have to stand back and fold their hands because they can't act on that. They can't act on words of fear. They can't act on words of failure.

The angels hearken to the Word of God (Psalm 103:20). When you speak words declaring God is your refuge and you speak the 91st Psalm out of your mouth, you empower the angels to enforce those words.

Your angels are with you. Give them words to work with.

Father, thank You for the wonderful protection that I enjoy 24 hours a day. Thank You, Lord, Your angels encompass me to deliver me. Your Word says they bear me up lest I dash my foot against a stone.

Thank You for my angelic security force.

> *The Angel of the Lord encamps around those who fear Him [who revere and worship Him with awe] and each of them He delivers.*
>
> PSALM 34:7
> *THE AMPLIFIED BIBLE*
>
> *Are not the angels all ministering spirits (servants) sent out in the service [of God for the assistance] of those who are to inherit salvation?*
>
> HEBREWS 1:14
> *THE AMPLIFIED BIBLE*

GLORIA COPELAND

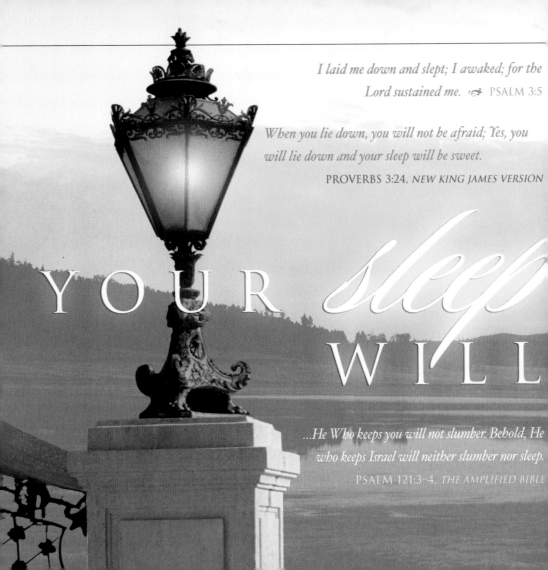

I laid me down and slept; I awaked; for the Lord sustained me. PSALM 3:5

When you lie down, you will not be afraid; Yes, you will lie down and your sleep will be sweet.
PROVERBS 3:24, *NEW KING JAMES VERSION*

YOUR *sleep* WILL

...He Who keeps you will not slumber. Behold, He who keeps Israel will neither slumber nor sleep.
PSALM 121:3-4, *THE AMPLIFIED BIBLE*

Y ou need to read the 91st Psalm at night before you go to bed.

Believe the things God says about your protection, and it will dislodge fear and insecurity from your life. It will enable you to go to sleep at night instead of staying awake and worrying.

God gives His angels charge over you to defend and preserve you. They set up camp wherever you are.

God and the angels are staying up, so you go ahead and sleep!

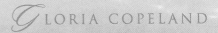

GLORIA COPELAND

I will both lay me down in peace, and sleep: for thou, Lord, only makest me dwell in safety. ✥ PSALM 4:8

BE SWEET

Tell the Lord, *"Lord, You're my refuge.*

"My trust is in You. I don't look to anything else to deliver me but You. I am going to close my eyes tonight and go to sleep, because I trust in You to keep me."

When the trouble

You shall tread upon the lion and adder;
the young lion and the serpent shall you trample underfoot.

PSALM 91:13 ❦ THE AMPLIFIED BIBLE

Word goes in, gets out.

Behold! I have given you authority and power to trample upon serpents and scorpions, and [physical and mental strength and ability] over all the power that the enemy [possesses]; and nothing shall in any way harm you.

LUKE 10:19
THE AMPLIFIED BIBLE

You have power and authority over the devil in every situation that he produces and over all the power that he possesses. Nothing shall in any way harm you.

When a challenge arises, release your authority. Say, "No, devil, I'll not have it that way. No, you can't do that, in the Name of Jesus."

Now, the Scripture doesn't say you won't have trouble. In fact, it says, *"Many are the afflictions of the righteous, But the Lord delivers him out of them all"* (Psalm 34:19, *New King James Version*).

You will always come out of trouble when you act on the Word of God.

GLORIA COPELAND

No room
FOR ANYTHING

Because he has set his love upon Me, therefore will I deliver him; I will set him on high, because he knows and understands My name [has a personal knowledge of My mercy, love, and kindness—trusts and relies on Me, knowing I will never forsake him, no, never].

PSALM 91:14 *THE AMPLIFIED BIBLE*

BUT GOD

When we set our love upon God, He delivers us.

This is His promise to those who will let God be God in their lives and who will walk in the fear and the honor of God enough to do what He says.

The reason God can deliver this person and put him under His protection and under His shadow is this person knows some things. When the devil comes to lie to him, he knows something different. He doesn't accept the lie. He knows God says, *"I will never forsake him, no never."*

You get that way by putting the Word of God concerning the mercies and the goodness of God in your ears and in your eyes. You become convinced of these things by spending time in His Word and by keeping it in front of your eyes. This gets His Word in the midst of your heart (Proverbs 4:20-27).

When your heart is full of His truth, there is no room for anything except knowledge of God and His goodness.

GLORIA COPELAND

He's
waiting for

He shall **call upon** Me,
and I will answer him; *I will be*
with him in trouble, I will deliver him and honor him.
PSALM 91:15 ❧ *THE AMPLIFIED BIBLE*

I will call upon the Lord, who is worthy to be praised:
so shall I be saved from mine enemies.  PSALM 18:3

In the day of my trouble I will call upon thee:
for thou wilt answer me. 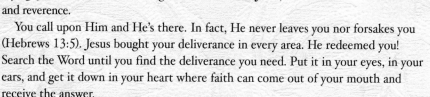 PSALM 86:7

your call

When you made Jesus Christ the Lord of your life, He became your Lord and your Savior.

Savior from what? Savior from sin. Savior from sickness. Savior from death. Savior from anything you need saving from.

In times of trouble you can call His Name, and you have just prayed Psalm 91, if you've called it in faith. You've just prayed your deliverance by saying "Jesus" in faith, not in slang as the world uses "Jesus," but in honor and reverence.

You call upon Him and He's there. In fact, He never leaves you nor forsakes you (Hebrews 13:5). Jesus bought your deliverance in every area. He redeemed you! Search the Word until you find the deliverance you need. Put it in your eyes, in your ears, and get it down in your heart where faith can come out of your mouth and receive the answer.

Then call Him Savior. Call Him Refuge. Call Him Deliverer. Call Him Healer.

Just call Him—He will answer!

GLORIA COPELAND

LIVE LONG

Live A LONG, RICH, HEALTHY, PROTECTED LIFE.

God's will is for you to make Him your refuge, for you to sit with Him in the place of protection and safety, and to live out the full number of your days on the earth.

You ought to live to be 80 or 90. Then, if you're not satisfied, live a while longer. God says, *"With long life will I satisfy him and show him My salvation"*—show him My deliverance, show him My protection, show him My prosperity, show him My healing, show him My wholeness.

You read about the patriarchs of the Bible, and it says they lived a long life, they died prosperous, they died satisfied, and they went to be with their fathers.

What a plan!

I thank You, Lord, that I'm going to walk out this life and live the full number of my days, or until You catch me away, and I'm going to do it without fear. I'm going to walk in faith. I'm going to walk in deliverance. I'm going to walk in abundance, I'm going to walk in health, and I'm going to walk in obedience and give You glory, Lord, for all the good You continually do in my life. To You be all the glory, in Jesus' Name. Amen.

GLORIA COPELAND

& SATISFIED

With long life will I satisfy him and show him My salvation.
PSALM 91:16 ❧ *THE AMPLIFIED BIBLE*

You shall serve the Lord your God....I will fulfill the number of your days.
EXODUS 23:25-26 ❧ *THE AMPLIFIED BIBLE*

ONE WORD

God is to us a God of deliverances and salvation; and to God the

Lord belongs escape from death [setting us free].

PSALM 68:20 ❧ *THE AMPLIFIED BIBLE*

In God is my salvation and my glory: the rock of my strength,

and my refuge, is in God.

PSALM 62:7

SAYS IT ALL

Salvation belongs to the Lord....

PSALM 3:8
*NEW KING
JAMES VERSION*

S alvation covers everything in your life that you need.

The word *salvation* includes your protection. In the Greek it denotes "deliverance, preservation, material and temporal deliverance from danger and apprehension [fear]." It means "pardon, protection, liberty, health, rest, restoration, soundness, wholeness." This word in the Greek means the same as the word in the Hebrew covenant for peace—*shalom*—nothing missing, nothing broken.

So your salvation includes freedom from fear. It includes your well-being in every area.

The Scripture says, *"Salvation belongs to the Lord."* The Lord has established Himself as the One who is responsible for your soundness, your deliverance, your protection, your blessing, your prosperity.

He has taken His place as your God. Now take your place as His protected child by the choices you make.

GLORIA COPELAND

Your _is_

_Who are being guarded (garrisoned)
by God's power through [your] faith...._
1 PETER 1:5 ❦ THE AMPLIFIED BIBLE

_...Be not slothful, but followers of them who
through faith and patience inherit the promises._
HEBREWS 6:12

NEED *already* MET

Your protection is not something you have to talk God into the notion of doing. It's something He has already provided for. Your part is simply to trust Him.

Scripture says in 1 Peter that we are guarded by God *through our faith*. Every part of our salvation comes to us by faith.

So let faith in His loving protection come into your heart today. Meditate the Word concerning your protection from danger.

Receive and rest in the care of a heavenly Father who met your need before you knew you had it.

GLORIA COPELAND

Don't give double up!

…We ought to pay much closer attention than ever to the truths that we have

heard, lest in any way we drift past [them] and slip away….

How shall we escape…if we neglect and refuse to pay attention

to such a great salvation [as is now offered to us, letting it drift past us forever]?

Hebrews 2:1, 3 *THE AMPLIFIED BIBLE*

up ...

Therefore we ought to give the more earnest heed to the things which we have heard, lest at any time we should let them slip.... How shall we escape, if we neglect so great salvation....

HEBREWS 2:1, 3

W e've had much pain and many problems in the United States in recent months. Unprecedented terrorism has come to America. In light of this, I was thinking about Psalm 91, when I heard these words in my spirit: *You have to hold your place there.*

Our protection is not automatic. It's not going to work for us if we're talking fear and doubt. We must speak what God says concerning these things. We must make our words line up with God's words by putting them in our hearts. When we put the Word of God in our heart in abundance, His Word will come out of our mouths.

In times like these, double up on the Word of God. Meditate twice as much on the Word. Do twice as much of the Word. Pray twice as much. Give twice as much.

This is a time to be bold, not a time to shrink back.

Be strong on the Word of God and stay there! Listen to tapes. Look up scriptures in the Bible about your deliverance and your protection.

Hold your place in Psalm 91.

Don't give up...*double up!*

GLORIA COPELAND

Not even the

Have You not made a hedge

around him

[Job], around his

household, and

around all that he

has on every side?

JOB 1:10 ❧ *NEW KING JAMES VERSION*

For I, saith the Lord, will be unto her [Jerusalem] a wall of fire round

smell of smoke

In the secret place of the Most High, it's as though God puts a wall around us.

That's why Shadrach, Meshach and Abednego did not smell like smoke when they came out of the fiery furnace. They had a wall around them. They were circled about by God.

Daniel 3:27 says, *"And the princes, governors, and captains, and the king's counsellors, being gathered together, saw these men, upon whose bodies the fire had no power, nor was an hair of their head singed, neither were their coats changed, nor the smell of fire had passed on them."*

They were covered and crowned with glory and honor. They were covered with the presence of God. There was an angel in there with them. And when they came out, they were so well covered that they didn't even smell like smoke. Not one thread of their clothes was scorched, not one hair on their head singed, because they were covered with His presence. They were covered with His glory. They were covered with His protection.

That's the kind of power we have available to us.

GLORIA COPELAND

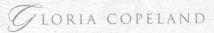 about, and will be the glory in the midst of her. ZECHARIAH 2:5

He who would love life and see

good days, let him refrain his

tongue from evil, and his lips

from speaking deceit.

1 PETER 3:10
NEW KING JAMES VERSION

Neither give place to the devil.

EPHESIANS 4:27

Leave no [such] room or

foothold for the devil [give no

opportunity to him].

EPHESIANS 4:27
THE AMPLIFIED BIBLE

MAKE IT

difficult
FOR THE *devil*

G od wants the hedge to always be up for our protection, the walls to always be up around us.

That is why He doesn't want us to speak words of defeat. He doesn't want us to speak words of trouble and take it on ourselves. He wants us to refrain our tongue from evil.

We speak God's Words. We speak in agreement with Him. We live in agreement with Him. We think in agreement with Him. We walk in agreement with Him.

How do we get like that? By spending time in the Word of God and getting it in our hearts in abundance. By putting it first place in our lives. By doing what it says.

The more we walk in agreement with Him, the more secure we are in this life and the more opportunities are taken away from the devil to cause us trouble.

Above

it all

No weapon that is formed
against thee shall prosper;
and every tongue that shall
rise against thee in judg-
ment thou shalt condemn.
This is the heritage of the
servants of the Lord,
and their righteousness
is of me, saith the Lord.

ISAIAH 54:17

Lord, I thank You for my divine protection. I thank You that no devil, person, nation, or great army of any size can ever overcome You. So I rest in You.

My life is hid with Christ in God. I dwell in the secret place of the Most High. It is written that I shall remain stable and fixed and no calamity will come near my tent. No plague will come near my dwelling. No curse of any kind is legal for me.

I walk in the blessing and I worship You, the Most High God! I thank You, Lord, that nothing can overcome You in my life! I thank You for the Holy Spirit who teaches me, counsels me and strengthens me in order that I walk with You according to Your Word.

I give You all honor and glory for all the good that You always do in my life. I have no fear of the future. Amen.

GLORIA COPELAND

refuse

...Thou shalt be far from oppression; for thou shalt not fear: and from terror; for it shall not come near thee. ❧ ISAIAH 54:14

TO FEAR

Father, I make You my refuge and my fortress. I give myself over into Your hands to be cared for, to be protected.

Because I have faith in Your Word, I refuse to have fear, Lord, concerning my future finances and my future health.

I refuse fear over the future of my nation and fear concerning terrorists and things of that nature. You said no weapon formed against me will prosper, and I shall be far from oppression and terror, for it shall not come near me.

You've given me witness after witness that I can walk through the flood and come out on the other side. I can walk through the fire and not be burned. I have the protection of the Most High.

I pray over every member of my family. I pray for their well-being, and I pray for the revelation of the Word of God to come to them and be plain to them concerning these things. I pray for the health and deliverance of every person in my family.

I thank You, Lord, that I have nothing to fear. I refuse to fear. I refuse to fear in the Name of Jesus.

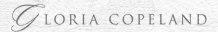

GLORIA COPELAND

Say this:

I do not receive fear. I rebuke fear, and in the Name of Jesus, I will never allow it back. If fear tries to come on me, I take authority over it and I resist it in the Name of Jesus. I have faith every day. I consider every day a day the Lord has made. I give myself to Him. I won't dread, I won't fear, and I won't sorrow in the Name of the Lord Jesus Christ.

Plead

And they overcame him
by the blood of the Lamb,
and by the word of their testimony.... REVELATION 12:11

Forasmuch as ye know that ye were not **redeemed**

with corruptible things, as silver and gold, from your vain

conversation received by tradition from your fathers; but

with the precious blood of Christ,
as of a lamb without blemish and without spot. 1 PETER 1:18-19

the blood

The only way to live in this crazy, mixed-up world is to spend time with God every morning before you get out there.

Plead the blood of Jesus. Say, *The Lord is my refuge and my fortress. I'm under the blood of Jesus, glory to God!*

Make this stand: *I'm covered in the blood of Jesus. Lord, I thank You that my whole family, my children, my grandchildren, my husband, my parents, my brothers and sisters and their families are all under the blood of Jesus. We are a family without tragedy.*

Start off your day with words like that. Don't get up in the morning expecting bad things to happen to you. Get up in the morning with the Word of God in your heart. God ought to be the first thing you think of when you wake up.

The blood of Jesus pushes back anything. Place it over your family, yourself and everyone you're connected with, and believe God for divine protection.

John G. Lake said, "There never was a devil in the world that ever went through the blood of Jesus, if the individual was in Christ." [1]

Today and every day, plead the blood.

*G*LORIA COPELAND

---

[1] *John G. Lake His Life, His Sermons, His Boldness of Faith*, Kenneth Copeland Publications. 1994.

God is our refuge and strength, a very present help in trouble.  PSALM 46:1

Protection

SCRIPTURES

Learn to take refuge in God.
Under the shadow of His wings you'll find peace,
security, safety and freedom from fear.

Genesis 18:14	Psalm 32:10	Proverbs 18:10	Ephesians 4:27
Exodus 14:19	Psalm 34:7	Proverbs 19:23	Ephesians 6:17
Exodus 23:25-26	Psalm 34:19	Proverbs 30:5	Philippians 2:10
Exodus 33:21	Psalm 37:23	Isaiah 26:3	Colossians 3:3
Deuteronomy	Psalm 37:39-40	Isaiah 41:10, 13	1 Thessalonians
30:19	Psalm 46:1	Isaiah 51:16	5:23
Joshua 1:8	Psalm 46:7	Isaiah 54:10	2 Thessalonians 3:3
Job 1:10	Psalm 57:1	Isaiah 54:14	2 Timothy 1:7
Psalm 3:5	Psalm 61:3-4	Isaiah 54:17	Hebrews 1:14
Psalm 3:8	Psalm 62:7	Isaiah 58:8	Hebrews 2:1, 3
Psalm 4:8	Psalm 68:20	Daniel 3:27	Hebrews 4:12
Psalm 5:11-12	Psalm 86:7	Zechariah 2:5	Hebrews 6:12
Psalm 17:8	Psalm 90:1	Matthew 23:37	Hebrews 13:5
Psalm 18:3	Psalm 91	Mark 11:23	1 Peter 1:5
Psalm 23:1	Psalm 94:22	Luke 10:19	1 Peter 1:18-19
Psalm 23:6	Psalm 119:114	Luke 21:9	1 Peter 3:10
Psalm 25:12-13	Psalm 120:3-4	John 15:7	1 John 2:24-25
Psalm 27:1, 5	Psalm 145:9	Romans 8:31	Revelation 12:11
Psalm 27:11	Psalm 145:18-19	1 Corinthians 1:9	
Psalm 31:1-3	Proverbs 3:5-6	2 Corinthians 4:13	
Psalm 31:19-20	Proverbs 3:24	2 Corinthians 6:17-18	
Psalm 32:7	Proverbs 14:26	2 Corinthians 12:9	

The Lord is my Shepherd

[to feed, guide, and shield

me], I shall not lack.

PSALM 23:1
THE AMPLIFIED BIBLE

A PRAYER FOR

Protection

We trust You with our lives today, Lord. You are our Shepherd. You are everything to us. We give You honor and praise. You are God to us.

We ask You for divine protection. We say, "You are our refuge and our fortress. You are our God and in You do we trust." We thank You for sending the angels to deliver us and to protect us.

A thousand might fall at our side, ten thousand at our right hand, but it won't come near us because You are our refuge. We abide under Your shadow, and we serve You, Lord.

We give You all the honor and all the praise. We plead the blood of Jesus for the protection of every person and every family represented by those who read this book. Lord, we're so thankful that we can trust You with our lives. We look to You. You're everything to us! You are our rock, Jesus! You are our life.

GLORIA COPELAND

Prayer
for Salvation
& Baptism in the
Holy Spirit

Heavenly Father, I come to You in the Name of Jesus. Your Word says, "Whosoever shall call on the name of the Lord shall be saved" (Acts 2:21). I am calling on You. I pray and ask Jesus to come into my heart and be Lord over my life according to Romans 10:9-10. "If thou shalt confess with thy mouth the Lord Jesus, and shalt believe in thine heart that God hath raised him from the dead, thou shalt be saved. For with the heart man believeth unto righteousness; and with the mouth confession is made unto salvation." I do that now. I confess that Jesus is Lord, and I believe in my heart that God raised Him from the dead.

I am now reborn! I am a Christian—a child of Almighty God! I am saved! You also said in Your Word, "If ye then, being evil, know how to give good gifts unto your children: HOW MUCH MORE shall your heavenly Father give the Holy Spirit to them that ask him?" (Luke 11:13). I'm also asking You to fill me with the Holy Spirit. Holy Spirit, rise up within me as I praise God. I fully expect to speak with other tongues as You give me the utterance (Acts 2:4). In Jesus' Name. Amen!

Begin to praise God for filling you with the Holy Spirit. Speak those words and syllables you receive—not in your own language, but the language given to you by the Holy Spirit. You have to use your own voice. God will not force you to speak. Don't be concerned with how it sounds. It is a heavenly language!

Continue with the blessing God has given you and pray in the spirit every day.

You are a born-again, Spirit-filled believer. You'll never be the same!

Find a good church that boldly preaches God's Word and obeys it. Become part of a church family who will love and care for you as you love and care for them.

We need to be connected to each other. It increases our strength in God. It's God's plan for us.

Make it a habit to watch the *Believer's Voice of Victory* television broadcast and become a doer of the Word, who is blessed in his doing (James 1:22-25).

OTHER PRODUCTS ABOUT GOD'S PROTECTION BY GLORIA COPELAND

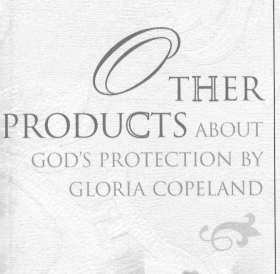